HEAVEN'S POWER
FOR THE HARVEST

HEAVEN'S POWER FOR THE HARVEST

BE PART OF GOD'S END-TIME SPIRITUAL OUTPOURING

by

Lynne Hammond

Harrison House
Tulsa, Oklahoma

06 05 04 03   10 9 8 7 6 5 4 3 2

Heaven's Power for the Harvest—
Be Part of God's End-Time Spiritual Outpouring
ISBN 1-57794-394-5 (formerly ISBN 1-57794-276-0)
Copyright © 2001 by Lynne Hammond
Mac Hammond Ministries
P.O. Box 29469
Minneapolis, MN 55429

Published by **Harrison House, Inc.**
P.O. Box 35035
Tulsa, Oklahoma 74153

CONTENTS

INTRODUCTION

Someone once related an interesting incident to me involving an eighteenth-century evangelist named John Whittier. The incident has stuck in my mind as an apt analogy of the church of Jesus Christ in these last days.

Whittier was a mighty preacher who lived in the early colonies after coming over to America from England. One day he and an Indian companion stood together before the great Niagara Falls, listening to the thunder of the massive waters as they crashed down into the canyon below.

Whittier said later that all he could hear was the thunderous roar of the waters. But suddenly the Indian pulled on his sleeve and said, "I hear an enemy coming."

Whittier turned to him and asked in wonder, "How do you know there's an enemy coming?"

The Indian replied, "Because I just heard a twig snap." The Indian's alertness saved the two men that day from the attack of an enemy Whittier didn't even know was near.

In the same way, I believe the church of Jesus Christ needs a wake-up call. I'm concerned in my heart that we're missing the cry of a lost world, as we allow the noise and clamor of the world to drown it out. Beneath the hustle and bustle, the jet engines and the materialism, the pleasures and all the "stuff" we think we have to do—beneath it all is a cry from the heart of God for the world.

So if I could ask the Lord to do only one thing for you through this book, I would ask Him to begin the same work in your heart that He has already begun in mine. He makes me very uncomfortable inside whenever I start becoming more concerned about supplying my own needs than I am about having a heart for lost souls.

Now, I don't know how God is going to put His heart-cry for the lost within His church. But I do know that He is big and smart and wise. He'll find a way. It's in His plan for this hour.

Meanwhile, I'm not satisfied anymore with just praying, "Lord, bless the world." I want to see the world as the Father sees it. And if I can help His plans for this generation come to pass by praying, then that's what I want to do.

The truth is, <u>we were all created to pray God's plans and purposes into being</u>. Just consider Jesus, who is our example. <u>Every step</u> of the way as He walked on this earth, <u>Jesus prayed</u>.

It was crucial for Jesus to pray during His life and ministry, and certainly it has always been crucial for the church of Jesus Christ to pray. But now in these last days, more than ever, it is time for the church to pray.

God wants to invade the earth with His power and glory beyond anything we could ask, dream or imagine. But we are the ones who will usher in that divine invasion, as we are faithful to pray according to the heart of our loving Father!

—*Lynne Hammond*

And the Lord answered me and said,
Write the vision and engrave it so plainly
upon tablets that everyone who
passes may [be able to] *read* [it easily
and quickly] *as he hastens by.*

HABAKKUK 2:2

1

THE VISION OF THE
DIVINE INVASION

1

THE VISION OF THE DIVINE INVASION

Every year on the same weekend in June, I attend a ladies' meeting in Paynesville, Minnesota. I've only missed three meetings since it started in 1980. I was called of God and separated to the ministry in one of those Paynesville meetings. It was the first time I ever saw the glory of God.

I go to that meeting every year not because it's a ladies' meeting, but because

God has never failed to meet me there. Every time I attend, I can always sense the presence of the Lord moving upon me strongly during the service.

Caught Up in the Spirit

A few years ago, I had an especially remarkable encounter with God during one of these meetings. The way it came about was so wonderful, and I haven't been the same since.

I'll never forget how it happened. When the service first began, I was a little distracted. I just couldn't seem to settle down.

But I've found the Lord knows exactly what to do to settle us down and get our attention when He wants to talk to us! That night He got my attention when I recalled in my heart words I'd heard Dr. Oral Roberts speak:

You are a book not yet published. You are a poem not yet recited. You are a song not yet sung. You are a dream not yet fulfilled. You are a vision that hasn't happened yet. You are a future that hasn't been fulfilled. You are a miracle about to happen.

I took this word to mean that this was not just for me, but for the entire body of Christ.

Then suddenly, I lost the awareness of my natural

YOU ARE A BOOK NOT YET PUBLISHED. YOU ARE A POEM NOT YET RECITED. YOU ARE A SONG NOT YET SUNG. YOU ARE A DREAM NOT YET FULFILLED. YOU ARE A VISION THAT HASN'T HAPPENED YET. YOU ARE A FUTURE THAT HASN'T BEEN FULFILLED. YOU ARE A MIRACLE ABOUT TO HAPPEN.
ORAL ROBERTS

surroundings and was caught up in the spirit. There I saw with my spiritual eyes what I can only describe as a great invasion of God in the earth.

I was thrilled as I looked at the unfolding of God's plan for the earth in the coming days.

In this vision, I wasn't just seeing a demonstration of God's glory in a local revival. I was witnessing an outpouring of the Spirit that reached to the ends of the world! I was watching a divine interruption of God in the earth—a literal invasion from heaven into the affairs of mankind.

Past and Present Invasions of God

After the vision, I began to look for books I could read about the subject of invasions. I was trying to find the words I needed to tell Christians how to pray. You see, I knew this divine invasion is exactly what it will take for God's purposes to be fulfilled in these last days. But I also realized we will have to pray this invasion into place to see it come to pass.

> DIVINE INVASION IS EXACTLY WHAT IT WILL TAKE FOR GOD'S PURPOSES TO BE FULFILLED IN THESE LAST DAYS.

I prayed, "Lord, You have to give me expression for what You have shown me in this vision. Please give me the words to speak of it accurately."

About that time, a book called *Invasion of Wales by the Spirit* caught my attention because it had that word *invasion* on the front cover. The book tells about the move of the Holy Spirit that swept Wales and changed the whole nation earlier this century.

I thought hopefully, *Well, this book might help me articulate what God showed me in that vision.*

In the book, I found one page that sounded a little like my vision, so I have decided to share it with you:

It was plainly evident now to everybody that God had entered the agonizing prayers of His people and had sent a mighty spiritual upheaval. A sense of the Lord's presence was everywhere. His presence was felt in the homes, on the street, in the mines, the factories and school, and even in the drinking saloons.

So great was His presence felt that even the places of amusement and carousels became places of holy awe. Many were the instances of men entering taverns, ordering drinks and then turning on their heels and leaving them untouched. Wales up to this time was in the grip of a football fever, when tens of thousands of working class men thought and talked only of one thing; they gambled also on the result of the games. Now the famous football players themselves got converted and joined the open-air street meetings to testify what glorious things the Lord had done for them. Many of the teams were disbanded as the players got converted and the stadiums were empty.

Beneath the ground the miners gathered for worship and Bible study before they dispersed to the various sections of the mines. Even the children in the schools came under the spell of God.[1]

Today there are similar but smaller modern-day invasions occurring all over the world. For example, someone recently told me about a move of God in Gadsden, Alabama. It was there that a young high school boy stepped off a curb and was hit by a cement truck.

The boy was given up to die. The doctor said every bone on one side of his body was completely shattered, and bone fragments had cut into his internal organs. The boy also had multiple head injuries. The doctors gave him no hope to live.

---

[1] Stewart, James A. *Invasion of Wales by the Spirit.* Asheville: Gospel Projects, Inc., 1963

But the mother refused to believe that. She knelt down by the side of her child's bed and asked the Lord to touch him.

About two hundred high school children had come to the hospital in support of their seriously wounded friend. So the mother told the teenagers, "They are about to 'airvac' my son to Birmingham. When the helicopter lifts off the hospital roof with him in it, just raise your hands and begin to thank God for his healing."

So all the kids went up on the roof and watched the medical personnel carefully place their friend in the helicopter. Then as the helicopter lifted off, they all joined the mother in lifting their hands and praising God.

> IN AN INSTANT, MULTITUDES OF PEOPLE WERE TOUCHED BY GOD AND MIRACULOUSLY HEALED.

Suddenly the power of God fell on the hospital. In an instant, multitudes of people were touched by God and miraculously healed. This supernatural event turned the whole city upside down, and many people came to the Lord.

I recently heard of another "mini-invasion" from heaven as I watched a videotaped sermon of Rev. Oral Roberts. During his message, Brother Roberts began to talk about mass miracles. He said he had seen this type of supernatural occurrence three times in his ministry of healing. The power of God would fall in his meeting, and everyone there who was physically handicapped, blind or maimed would be totally healed.

Brother Roberts talked about one particular night when he was ministering to people in the healing line through the laying on of hands.

He said, "I could feel the touch of God on me, making me very aware of His presence. It was similar to a wind. But suddenly it was as if I was hit with that power. It hit me so hard that it made me call out, 'It's come! It's come! He's here!'"

When he said that, people from all over the building jumped out of their wheelchairs. People who were on crutches were totally healed. Blind eyes were opened. For the next twelve minutes, every sick or injured person in that place was totally and completely healed and delivered! Brother Roberts said that the mound of discarded crutches, wheelchairs and braces in the back of the tent after the service looked like a mountain!

GOD WANTS TO *INVADE* THIS PLANET WITH HIS POWER AND GLORY.

I'm ready for those kinds of supernatural occurrences to start happening all the time throughout the body of Christ! I love what God is doing all over this earth. But I'm not satisfied! God wants to *invade* this planet with His power and glory, and I want us to help Him do it!

For the vision is yet for an appointed time
and it hastens to the end [fulfillment];
it will not deceive or disappoint.
Though it tarry, wait [earnestly] *for it,*
because it will surely come; it will not be
behindhand on its appointed day.

HABAKKUK 2:3

2

"Lord, Revive
Your Works"

2

"LORD, REVIVE YOUR WORKS"

After the Lord gave me the vision of His coming invasion of this earth, I went to the Word for confirmation. I knew if the vision was of God, it had to line up with the Word.

I found a passage of Scripture in the book of Habakkuk that reminds me of what I saw in the vision. Before we read it, let me explain that Habakkuk was a seer, someone to whom

God would show things that were to come. And in a very real sense, God has made all of us in the body of Christ to be seers.

We should all be sensitive enough to the Holy Spirit's guidance to see out ahead of us. God wants us to set our sights on the future instead of allowing our minds to park indefinitely in the "parking lot" of the past. If we choose to do the latter, we will go nowhere spiritually and remain oblivious to both the devil's strategies and our role in God's plan for this hour.

> WE SHOULD ALL BE SENSITIVE ENOUGH TO THE HOLY SPIRIT'S GUIDANCE TO SEE OUT AHEAD OF US.

Habakkuk's Vision
of a Divine Invasion

In Habakkuk 2, the seer talks about a time the Lord gave him a profound vision:

> [Oh, I know, I have been rash to talk out plainly this way to God!] I will [in my thinking] stand upon my post of observation and station myself on the tower or fortress, and will watch to see what He will say within me and what answer I will make.

> **Habakkuk 2:1**

Habakkuk said, "I will stand upon my post of observation." I believe that we as Christians haven't been standing enough on *our* post of observation. Our eyes are too dim. They're too fixed on the things of this world. The Father is trying to show us His vision and His plans for this hour, but spiritually we're not paying close enough attention.

We should strive to be like Habakkuk, who stood on his observation post and said, "I will watch to see what God will say within me and what answer I will make," I'm telling you, we need to wake up, because there is coming a day when every one of us will answer to the Lord!

This was God's answer to Habakkuk:

And the Lord answered me and said, Write the vision and engrave it so plainly upon tablets that everyone who passes may [be able to] read [it easily and quickly] as he hastens by.

For the vision is yet for an appointed time and it hastens to the end [fulfillment]; it will not deceive or disappoint. Though it tarry, wait [earnestly] for it, because it will surely come; it will not be behindhand on its appointed day.

Habakkuk 2:2,3

Verses 13-14 go on to tell us about the vision Habakkuk saw as he stood on his observation tower, waiting for the Lord to show him what He wanted His prophet to see. This is the vision God wanted him to write down and engrave upon his heart.

Behold, is it not by appointment of the Lord of hosts that the nations toil only to satisfy the fire [that will consume their work], and the peoples weary themselves only for emptiness, falsity, and futility?

But [the time is coming when] the earth shall be filled with the knowledge of the glory of the Lord as the waters cover the sea.

This last verse describes the divine invasion I saw in the spiritual realm very well!

Habakkuk's Response to the Vision: Prayer

Then in Habakkuk 3:2, we see Habakkuk the prophet praying as a result of the vision he received of the earth filled with the power and the glory of the Lord.

> **O Lord, I have heard the report of You and was afraid.** *O Lord, revive Your work* **in the midst of the years, in the midst of the years make [Yourself] known! In wrath [earnestly] remember love, pity, and mercy.**

Habakkuk began to pray that God would *revive His works.* Now, understand this: God doesn't have a bunch of little, anemic, trickling works; He has *mighty* works. Just go through the Bible, and you'll find that His works include things like parting the Red Sea and making the sun stand still!

GOD HAS
MIGHTY WORKS.

The Spirit of God hasn't toned down His method of operation since the days of Habakkuk or the book of Acts. The caliber of man that Habakkuk was hasn't ceased to exist on this earth. There are still many people who are on fire for God, who see and know what He wants to do in the future.

So Habakkuk prayed, "Revive Your works, Lord." In other words, he was saying, "Lord, make Yourself known not just to me; make Yourself known not only in the praise and worship services; but make Yourself known to those who dwell in the dark places of the earth."

THERE ARE SO MANY WHO WILL NEVER KNOW JESUS UNLESS THE CHURCH PRAYS.

That kind of prayer is so important. There are so many who will never know Jesus unless the church does what she is supposed to do and *prays*.

That's why I often check up on myself in this area. I ask, "God, am I like the husbandman in James 5:7 who waits for the precious fruit of the earth? Am I watching and praying for a harvest of souls to bring into Your kingdom, Father?"

We should all be asking God that same question. And if His answer is no, then we need to allow Him to adjust our hearts accordingly!

Habakkuk 3:3 goes on to say, **God [approaching from Sinai] came.…** Habakkuk saw in his vision that *God* came. He prayed, "Revive Your works, O Lord," and as a result, God came.

> WHAT HAPPENS IN THE REVIVING OF THE WORKS OF GOD? *GOD COMES.*

What happens in the reviving of the works of God? *God comes.* He comes into homes; He comes to the streets. And wherever He invades, everyone knows it. The vision Habakkuk saw in the realm of the spirit explains how He makes Himself known:

His glory covered the heavens and the earth was full of His praise. And His brightness was like the sunlight; rays streamed from His hand, and

there [in the sun like splendor] was the hiding place of His power.

Habakkuk 3:3,4

WHEN GOD COMES, THE BRIGHTNESS OF HIS GLORY SHINES LIKE RAYS OF SUNLIGHT INTO YOUR HOME.

When God comes, the brightness of His glory shines like rays of sunlight into your home, into your neighbor's home—into every home that lets Him in.

Then verse 5 says, **Before Him went the pestilence [as in Egypt], and burning plague followed His feet [as in Sennacherib's army].** When the flood of God comes, everything that is not of Him is washed up and washed out—everything! Nothing is left.

He stood and measured the earth; He looked and shook the nations; and the eternal mountains were scattered and the perpetual hills bowed low. His ways are everlasting and His goings are of old.

I [Habakkuk, in vision] saw the tents of Cushan [probably Ethiopia] in affliction; the [tent] curtains of the land of Midian trembled.

Habakkuk 3:6,7

Habakkuk said that the curtains of the land of Midian *trembled*. You see, God can shake cities and nations. He can do it, and I declare that He *will* do it!

Were You displeased with the rivers, O Lord? Or was Your anger against the rivers [You divided]? Was Your wrath against the [Red] Sea, that You rode [before] upon Your horses and Your chariots of victory and deliverance?

Your bow was made quite bare; sworn to the tribes [of Israel] by Your sure word were the rods of chastisement, scourges, and calamities.

Habakkuk 3:8,9

GOD KNOWS HOW
TO TAKE CARE OF
THE ENEMY!

I guarantee you, God knows how to take care of the enemy! He is the almighty God, and He knows just what to do to thwart the devil's attacks on His people.

With rivers You cleaved the earth [bringing forth waters in dry places]. The mountains saw You, they trembled and writhed [as if in pain]. The overflowing of the water passed by [as at the deluge]; the deep uttered its voice and lifted its hands on high.

The sun and moon stood back [as before Joshua] in their habitation at the light of Your arrows as they sped, at the flash of Your glittering spear.

You marched through the land in indignation, You trampled and threshed the nations in anger. You went forth and have come for the salvation of Your people, for the deliverance and victory of Your anointed [people Israel].

Habakkuk 3:9-13

Why does God invade this earth? For the deliverance and victory of His people!

Just keep reading Habakkuk 3, and you will catch a vision of what this

WHY DOES GOD INVADE THIS EARTH? FOR THE DELIVERANCE AND VICTORY OF HIS PEOPLE!

invasion of God entailed. In verse 16, Habakkuk described his own reaction to what he saw coming in the future:

> I heard and my [whole inner self] trembled; my lips quivered at the sound. Rottenness enters into my bones and under me [down to my feet]; I tremble. I will wait quietly for the day of trouble and distress when there shall come up against [my] people him who is about to invade and oppress them.

You see, Habakkuk realized he couldn't do anything in his own strength to avert the calamity to come. God was the only One who knew just how to fix the situation.

In the same way, God knows just how to bring you to the end of yourself—to the place where you finally admit you can't figure things out on your own and you start yielding to God. That's when you pray, "Lord, do something! Revive Your works in the midst of us!"

This is the day the Church of the Lord Jesus Christ is going to have to contend for some things in prayer. We must be known as contenders for the plans and the purposes of God. We need to go to our prayer closets no matter what else is going on around us, realizing that there will always be distractions trying to keep us from praying out the plan of God on this earth.

THERE WILL ALWAYS BE DISTRACTIONS TRYING TO KEEP US FROM PRAYING OUT THE PLAN OF GOD ON THIS EARTH.

That's one of the main things we can learn from the book of Habakkuk. When the prophet saw with his spiritual eyes what lay ahead in the future, what did he do? *He prayed.*

The Consequences of Failing To Pray

As I read about Habakkuk and his response to the vision God gave him, I'm reminded of the last missionary who came out of China before the communist regime took over. This missionary was a pastor, and just before he had to leave the country, he met with his congregation for the very last time.

The pastor walked up on the platform and turned to look at his congregation. Outside they could hear the marching feet of communist armies on their way to take over the land.

Then the pastor asked, "Whose fault is it that the communist regime is taking over? Whose fault is it that they are here? Is it the government's fault? No, it's not the government's fault; it's *our* fault. The blame lies right here. The reason I have to leave you tomorrow is that we did nothing in prayer to stop this."

WE DID NOTHING IN PRAYER TO STOP THIS.

The pastor's words are a sobering reminder of the importance of prayer. So now let's apply it to the day we live in. What if the church doesn't pray for God's plans to come to pass in this hour? If the church fails to pray, perhaps instead of a divine invasion in the next ten years, we may find ourselves, like those Chinese believers, under the rule of oppression!

Showing Us Things To Come

We have seen how God showed Habakkuk things that would happen in the future. Can we, as believers, expect God to do the same thing for us? We absolutely can! In John 16:13 KJV, Jesus told us that was one of the things the Holy Spirit would do in our lives :

Howbeit when he, the Spirit of truth, is come, he will guide you into all truth: for he shall not speak of himself; but whatsoever he shall hear, that shall he speak: and he will shew you things to come.

As Jesus promised, the Holy Spirit has come to dwell in our midst and to live within us. He is called the Spirit of Truth, and He has come not only to guide us into truth, but to show us things that are to come.

That means the Lord is not just interested in helping us understand what's going on in this present moment. The Spirit of God living inside of us is also very interested in our knowing about the *future*.

So release your faith to receive that supernatural knowledge, and allow the

RELEASE YOUR FAITH TO RECEIVE SUPERNATURAL KNOWLEDGE, AND ALLOW THE HOLY SPIRIT TO BEGIN TO SHOW YOU THINGS TO COME.

Holy Spirit to begin to show you things to come. John 16:13 is yours to claim, because you are a child of God and you belong to Jesus.

The Church of Jesus Christ— A Praying Church

The Holy Spirit shows you that which is to come so you can both *declare* God's future purposes in faith and *pray* that those divine purposes would come to pass. That's just the way God operates.

If you study the Bible from the beginning to the end, you'll see a pattern. Before God does something, He tells His people what He's going to do. He does this so they will begin believing for it, declaring it and praying about it in faith.

One of God's most difficult challenges is to get us to fulfill our responsibility to pray about what He has shown us. We all want to hear what He has to say, but we *don't* all want to get on our knees and pray about it.

> BEFORE GOD DOES SOMETHING, HE TELLS HIS PEOPLE WHAT HE'S GOING TO DO.

Second Chronicles 7:14 KJV says,

If my people, which are called by my name, shall humble themselves, and pray, and seek my face, and turn from their wicked ways; then will I hear from heaven, and will forgive their sin, and will heal their land.

Notice that this divine promise is conditional. God says, "*If* My people who are called by My name will humble themselves and pray, I will heal their land." The healing of the land comes only when God's people humble themselves and pray.

The truth is, America is probably the most arrogant nation in the world. Unfortunately, that spirit of pride has entered the church as well.

> AMERICA IS PROBABLY THE MOST ARROGANT NATION IN THE WORLD.

Too many of us think we can bring in the end-time harvest by implementing our own programs instead of getting on our knees to pray. But the fact is, we can't. We can't cause a divine invasion to take place in our own strength. Only God can do that.

Only God can send a healing revival. Only God can clean out a hospital of all its sick people. Only God can turn the hearts of rebellious teenagers back to Himself. Only God can take children out of abusive environments and put them in peaceful homes. Only God can do it, and I believe He *will* do it—*as we become willing and obedient to pray.*

*For My thoughts are not
your thoughts, neither are your
ways My ways, says the Lord.*

ISAIAH 55:8

3

GET HUNGRY FOR GOD

3

GET HUNGRY FOR GOD

I want to point out something else about the experience I had at that ladies' conference in Paynesville when the Spirit of God moved on me so strongly. Spiritual hunger was a key factor to the entire experience. Because I came to that conference hungry for more of God, He was able to prepare my heart for what He wanted to give me—the vision of His coming invasion.

You see, at an earlier meeting before the vision, we were all praying together corporately, and I got lost in the spirit. As I prayed, I began to sense the Lord doing something in me that I had wanted Him to do for a long time. I had been seeking Him for it. I was *hungry* for it.

You know, sometimes the Lord will catch you off guard. You may have been seeking Him diligently for something, praying, "God, will You do this? Lord, I want this so much. I need You to do this!" Then suddenly He just hits you with what you've been desiring when you don't expect it!

That night I entered a place in God I hadn't visited for a long time. And do you know what the result was? It made me even more hungry for Him. I didn't think I could get any hungrier, but I found out I could!

You see, there are degrees of hunger, both natural and spiritual. You can be just hungry enough to want to snack a little, or you can be so hungry that the thought of food consumes your mind.

I know what it feels like to be that hungry. Recently, as my family and I were on our way to a nearby lake, I realized I hadn't eaten all day. Ever since we had started the trip, I couldn't figure out why I was being so fidgety in the car. But then I realized the reason—I had forgotten to eat! And for the rest of the trip, I was so hungry for food that I couldn't think of anything else.

That's how hungry you should be for the things of God. For instance, when someone preaches by the anointing of God and the Holy Spirit starts moving, it should make you hungry for more of God in the same way a little one-course meal makes you hungry for more food.

YOU HAVE TO COME BEFORE HIS THRONE ON A DAILY BASIS AND GIVE YOURSELF TO PRAYER.

But do you know who can make you hungrier than anyone else? God can! That's why you have to come before His throne on a daily basis and give yourself to prayer. It's so important that you have seasons of prayer with God all by yourself.

You see, it's all well and good to come together corporately as a local body of believers and enjoy the presence of the Lord together. But it's not nearly as wonderful as it can be when God meets you alone in the intimacy of your own prayer closet.

Hunger Opens the Heart to God

So on this particular night at the ladies' conference, I came to a place in God where I hadn't been in a long time, and it made me so hungry for Him. And I stayed hungry all night! I stayed even hungrier the next day. As God kept making me more and more hungry, my heart started opening up wide to Him.

You see, when we don't hunger after spiritual things, our hearts can become closed and hardened toward God. The good news is, however, that God specializes in softening our closed, hard hearts by making Himself known to us.

The way our hearts sometimes get hard toward God reminds me of a turtle. A turtle has a hard shell on top of him, but underneath its body is soft and pliable.

> OUR HEARTS CAN GET COVERED UP WITH ALL SORTS OF THINGS.

Similarly, our hearts can get covered up with all sorts of things—family affairs, the circumstances of life, problems, bad attitudes and so on. If that happens, we won't be wide open when God knocks on the door of our hearts. The hard shell we have built around our hearts will keep us closed off from the joy of God's presence.

However, the moment we encounter the reality of God's presence even once, it softens our hearts and makes us hungry for another divine encounter. That's how powerful it is to experience firsthand the love and mercy of God!

> THE MOMENT WE ENCOUNTER THE REALITY OF GOD'S PRESENCE EVEN ONCE, IT SOFTENS OUR HEARTS AND MAKES US HUNGRY FOR ANOTHER DIVINE ENCOUNTER.

A New Heart for the Lost

So by the time I entered that service in which the Lord caught me up in the spirit, I was wide open to Him and hungry for more. And God was faithful to give me more. One of the things the Lord gave me that night through the vision was an even greater hunger for souls.

Through the years, God has given me a great burden for souls. But since God gave me the vision of His invasion, something new has been happening to me as I pray for the lost. I don't understand it all, but I'll try to explain it the best I can.

As I prayed in the past, the people were always descending in a downward spiral into the pit of darkness, and I was reaching for them in prayer, trying to grasp their hand with my hand to pull them out of the darkness. But since I saw that divine invasion, God has moved me into the midst of the lost souls as I pray. I have become one of them. We are all crying out to Him, but my cry is the loudest. I walk among the lost and cry out to God for them as the Spirit of God prays through me.

Through these experiences in prayer, I have come to understand that I am my brother's keeper. That's what comes up inside of me as the Holy Ghost prays through me. *I am my brother's keeper.*

> I AM MY BROTHER'S KEEPER.

And so are we all. You see, Judgment Day is coming—when all our works will be tried by fire, and all the "wood, hay and stubble" will be burned up. (1 Cor. 3:12,13.) Only the gold and silver of our works that endured will be left.

Do you ever wonder what your pile of gold and silver will look like? Will there only be a small pile of godly works left after the fire burns up the works of the flesh, or will there be a huge pile of gold to present to the Lord?

And what will we do when it's time for souls to be condemned to hell? What will it be like to stand there and watch as people are thrown into the lake of fire forever? Will we think, *Did I know any of them? Could I have done anything that would have kept them from going there?*

Becoming More Aware of Heaven Than of Earth

That question has become much more important to me than natural questions, such as whether or not the dog gets a bath this week. I've discovered that when you become truly hungry for God and revival comes to your heart, one thing that happens to you is that you become more aware of heaven than you are of earth. Everything on the other side of the veil becomes very, very real to you.

AS YOU PRAY, YOU LEARN TO MOVE FROM THIS EARTHLY REALM INTO THE REALM OF THE SPIRIT.

As you pray, you learn to move from this earthly realm into the realm of the Spirit, where you begin to see with the eyes of your heart "the city foursquare," in all of its light and glory. (Rev. 21.) Such experiences make you more and more hungry for God. They cause your mind to think less about natural things than you think about eternal things—including the destiny of lost souls.

You see, it's true that the Bible says our thoughts are not God's thoughts and our ways are not God's ways. (Isa. 55:8.) But it's also true that once we get saved, we can begin to learn to think the way God thinks and live according to His ways.

You can have God's thoughts. You can be delivered from the perils of the beggarly elements of this earth, including selfish, carnal thinking. God will help you do that. He will give you His desire to see all men saved.

Just continue to delight yourself in Him. Keep your heart wide open to His Spirit. And above all, *stay hungry* for more of Him!

You went forth and have come for the salvation of Your people, for the deliverance and victory of Your anointed [people Israel]; *You smote the head of the house of the wicked, laying bare the foundation even to the neck. Selah* [pause, and calmly think of that]!

4

PRAY FOR GOD'S COMING INVASION

4

PRAY FOR GOD'S COMING INVASION

God is about to invade this earth, and He has allowed us to see and hear about it before it happens. The Holy Spirit has declared it to us before it ever even comes!

In Habakkuk 3:13, God declares through His prophet the reason why He invades this earth: **You went forth and have come for the salvation of Your people, for the deliverance and victory of Your anointed [people Israel].**

GOD IS ONE
WHO DECLARES
THINGS.

You see, God is one who declares things. He loves to say, "I said this was going to happen. I declared it, and it came to pass." He also loves for His people to declare His promises in faith. It's a family trait God wants all His children to adopt as their own.

So I urge you to make a quality decision to begin to pray out God's plans for these last days. Start declaring in faith that what He has said *will* come to pass.

Now, when you hear the word *pray*, you may think of it as a dry exercise of drudgery and duty. But that isn't God's design for prayer. As you get hungry for God and begin to pray in the Spirit, you *will* connect with Him. And when you do, I guarantee you that it will be anything but dry drudgery!

> AS YOU GET HUNGRY FOR GOD AND BEGIN TO PRAY IN THE SPIRIT, YOU *WILL* CONNECT WITH HIM.

Just consider the time God told Moses to come to the mountain and meet Him there. God told Moses that He wanted to visit him. He wanted to make Himself real to Moses, and He wants to do the same for you. Therefore, the question isn't, "How can you get God to visit you?" It's, "How can God get you to *let* Him visit you?"

Finally, I want to urge you to find a good prayer group to join so you can learn to pray corporately with other believers. God likes it when His people gather together to pray. When believers come into God's presence in unity, amazing things can happen as God moves miraculously in their midst. While they have a Holy Ghost party in prayer, God goes forth to change the world!

So let this prayer come up out of your heart to the throne of God:

Lord, I ask You to visit me right now by Your Holy Spirit. I pray, Father, for Your manifested presence and glory in my life as I commit myself to pray out Your plans and purposes for the days and years ahead.

Father, help me make the necessary adjustments in my own life to fulfill Your call to pray. Thank You for Your presence in my life. Thank You for Your manifested glory in my city, my nation, my world.

I declare in faith that the invasion You have purposed to bring to this earth shall come to pass in Jesus' name!

ABOUT THE AUTHOR

Lynne Hammond is nationally known for her teaching and writing on the subject of prayer. The desire of Lynne's heart is to impart the spirit of prayer to churches and nations throughout the world. Her books include *Secrets to Powerful Prayer, When Healing Doesn't Come Easily, Dare To Be Free* and *The Master Is Calling*.

She is the host and teacher for *A Call to Prayer,* a weekly European television broadcast, and is an occasional guest teacher on her husband's national weekly television broadcast, *The Winner's Way With Mac Hammond.* She also regularly writes articles on the subject of prayer in *Winner's Way* magazine and publishes a newsletter called *Prayer Notes* for people of prayer. Lynne is a frequent speaker at national prayer conferences and meetings around the country.

Lynne and her husband, Mac, are founders of Living Word Christian Center, a large and growing church in Minneapolis, Minnesota. Under Lynne's leadership at Living Word, the prayer ministry has become a nationally recognized model for developing effective "pray-ers."

To contact Lynne Hammond,
write:

Lynne Hammond
Mac Hammond Ministries
P.O. Box 29469
Minneapolis, Minnesota 55429

*Please include your prayer requests
and comments when you write.*

OTHER BOOKS BY
LYNNE HAMMOND

Spiritual Enrichment Series:
Living in the Presence of God
When It's Time for a Miracle
Staying Faith

Secrets to Powerful Prayer:
Discovering the Languages of the Heart

When Healing Doesn't Come Easily

The Master Is Calling:
Discovering the Wonders of Spirit-Led Prayer

Dare To Be Free

Available from your local bookstore.

HARRISON HOUSE
Tulsa, Oklahoma 74153

Prayer of Salvation

God loves you—no matter who you are, no matter what your past. God loves you so much that He gave His one and only begotten Son for you. The Bible tells us that "…whoever believes in him shall not perish but have eternal life" (John 3:16 NIV). Jesus laid down His life and rose again so that we could spend eternity with Him in heaven and experience His absolute best on earth. If you would like to receive Jesus into your life, say the following prayer out loud and mean it from your heart.

Heavenly Father, I come to You admitting that I am a sinner. Right now, I choose to turn away from sin, and I ask You to cleanse me of all unrighteousness. I believe that Your Son, Jesus, died on the cross to take away my sins. I also believe that He rose again from the dead so that I might be forgiven of my sins and made righteous through faith in Him. I call upon the name of Jesus Christ to be the Savior and Lord of my life. Jesus, I choose to follow

You and ask that You fill me with the power of the Holy Spirit. I declare that right now I am a child of God. I am free from sin and full of the righteousness of God. I am saved in Jesus' name. Amen.

If you prayed this prayer to receive Jesus Christ as your Savior for the first time, please contact us on the web at <u>www.harrisonhouse.com</u> to receive a free book.

Or you may write to us at

Harrison House

P.O. Box 35035

Tulsa, Oklahoma 74153

If this book has been a blessing to you
or if you would like to see more of
the Harrison House product line,
please visit us on our website at
www.harrisonhouse.com.

The Harrison House Vision

Proclaiming the truth and the power

Of the Gospel of Jesus Christ

With excellence;

Challenging Christians to

Live victoriously,

Grow spiritually,

Know God intimately.